AF390797

HOW TO STAY SLIM WITHOUT DIETING ?

10 French Habits

Stephan Ducoup

ISBN : 978-2-9573722-1-8

CONTENTS

Author's Preface

How can French people eat gourmet dishes, cakes, breads, and cheeses, as well as drink wine, and at the same time stay slim?

Being French and living abroad, I've heard this question hundreds of times, especially when I was working in the US and in Japan. The mystery of "French Paradox" by excellence! Back to Paris, I founded fusion cooking restaurants, and my international customers used to ask me the same question.

I decided to write a book about French eating tips and tricks so I could explain to my foreign friends our secrets, which are actually more like habits. This book is far from being a scientific essay, but I will try to summarize French habits in terms of their lifestyle so readers can stay slim and healthy. I hope you'll enjoy reading it!

Bon appetit!

Introduction

How to stay slim without dieting ? French people are the best kind of people to answer this question.

The rest of the world often views France as a food paradise. We can find a very large selection of breads, cheeses, desserts, and other dishes. We all know that French people love spending time eating and drinking. On the other hand, French people are still among the slimmest in the EU as per the EUROSTAT IMC statistics. Also, in the OCDE statistics, we can see that France still has a low obesity rate compared to some industrialized countries, such as the US, Canada, and the UK. If we look at the obesity rate of French children, we can also see that those rates didn't increase much in the last 20 years.

So, what are the secrets of French eating habits? Is the French Paradox legend true?

Actually, if we look at the details, we realize that it's not about magic potions or extreme dieting. It's about the basic eating habits and lifestyle passed on from generation to generation.

So here are the ten main habits of French people that help them stay slim without dieting.

Habit 1

FRENCH TEMPO

One French secret is to eat everyday at the same time, three main meals a day, and a healthy snack the afternoon if necessary. This is not difficult, but we have to do it everyday! Nowadays, the rhythm of our life gives us fake excuses to eat anywhere, anytime. We often hear, "I don't have time to eat breakfast," or, "I was so busy at the office today that I didn't have time to eat lunch." If we live in big cities, it's very easy to grab food at any corner, any time of the day. We have lost the importance of eating meals. We need to find a balanced rhythm to eat so as to not snack all day long.

OK, let's go!

AT WHAT TIME DO FRENCH EAT?

The French eat three main dishes a day at about the same time everyday.

- **breakfast** around 8:00am

- **lunch** around 1:00pm

- **healthy snack** around 4:00pm

- **dinner** around 8:00pm

The French are conditioned to eat at a regular time everyday. From a young age, kids are taught to eat only during meal time and not between. The scholarly world follows this rule as well, and there are no classes usually between 12:00pm and 2:00pm so kids can take time to eat.

Generally, the tempo of the whole French society is built in accordance to meal times. The public television channels broadcast the main news at 1:00pm and 8:00pm everyday. People working in an office usually have a minimum of one hour to eat between 12:00pm and 2:00pm. Some administrations of public offices are closed during meal times. In small towns and villages, most of the shops will close during this time. Even in Paris, most of the restaurants are not open all the time but have restricted opened hours. Usually service hours are from 11:30am to 3:30pm for lunch and from 7:00pm to 11:30pm for dinner. Only a few brasseries stay open 24/7. So it's easy to see why it's more natural for the French to eat at the same time every day.

WHAT ARE THE MAIN FRENCH MEALS?

1 - Breakfast : «Le Petit Déjeuner»

"Breakfast" literally means "small lunch" in French. In France, we don't start the day with a fast break but instead with a slow, small lunch.

Traditional breakfast is rather sweet. It usually contains a hot drink, such as a black coffee, a tea, or a hot chocolate. Then bread, as the French are consistently the top consumers of baguettes. Bread is usually eaten in the style of la tartine. We cut slices of baguettes or bread and sometimes toast it. Then butter and jam are spread on top, and then we dip it into the hot drink to make it soft and creamy! Nowadays, wheat and cereal breads are becoming more and more popular. We also eat fruit, yogurt, and porridge. Some adults make a bigger breakfast with ham, cheese, and eggs! Kids usually drink hot chocolate, milk, or fruit juice, and they tend to eat cereal, like cornflakes.

During special occasions or on Sundays, families take more time to have breakfast together. Sometimes we eat pastries, like croissants, chocolate bread, and so on.

Why it is important to eat breakfast ?

Eating breakfast helps us acquire our daily dose of fiber, protein, calcium and vitamins to start the day with enough energy. When we start the day with energy, we will be able to avoid snacking during the morning.

When we eat breakfast, our body will record that we have enough calories to start the day. Our brain needs also some energy to run. Eating restores our glucose levels and helps our memory and attention to work properly all day long.

When we skip breakfast, our body will think it needs to store extra calories to start the day. Instead of burning it, it will make extra storage, which can cause weight gain. Also when we skip meals, our blood sugar levels can fluctuate, which may cause reactions like.: headache, loss of energy, bad moods…

2 - Lunch

Even if we sometimes hear, "We should eat breakfast like a king, lunch like a prince, and eat dinner like a pauper!", lunch is the main meal for French people. Lunch provides us more than 1/3 of our daily energy and helps us avoid afternoon snacking. In France, meals are sequenced and balanced.

Here is atypical lunch at home for French people.

1. **hors d'oeuvre:** usually raw vegetables, eggs, or small mixed salad

2. **main dish:** meat, fish, or cooked dish with a vegetable or green salad

3. **a lettuce salad** with homemade dressing (optional)

4. **cheese** (optional)

5. **dessert** which can be fruit or yogurt

6. **coffee** (optional)

Here are some **super food** ideas to include in our meal:
avocado, seeds, lettuce, apple, peas, pumpkin, walnuts, asparagus, tomatoes, whole wheat bread, salmon, egg, chicken, oatmeal…
We shouldn't forget to drink a lot of water and avoid sugary drinks.

3 - Snacking : « le quatre heures »

In France, the old tradition of tea time was called "le gouter," which means "tasting," but also "le quatre heures," as it usually takes place around 4:00pm. It's also the name of the healthy snack that growing kids eat to help them wait until the dinner. As usual, forget about junk food and prepare them a homemade cake or bread with chocolate or jam, fruit jam, dairy drinks, and fruit.

For adults, it's the only snack allowed. The French avoid junk food and instead have yogurt, fruit, or fruit jam. We drink water or juice without sugar added.

4 - Dinner

Dinner is the last time of the day when we should eat. The French generally eat around 8:00pm. It can be late compared to some European countries, but it's not as late as some Mediterranean neighbors. Dinner is lighter than lunch. The French tend to eat cereals, raw or cooked vegetables, and mixed salads, not dishes with sauces. The dinner can be a dish and a dessert for example:

- main dish: soup, pasta, rice, egg, vegetables, or salad

- dairy: cheese, yogurt, cottage cheese

- fruit

- a piece of bread as an option!

The French don't drink coffee or tea at night. They instead have herbals teas to help digest, relax, and sleep easily.

Tricks and Tips for Dinner

- **eat a light dinner**
  Our metabolism will slow down at night so, we should not eat big quantities of food for dinner. Eat light and avoid fatty foods. Heavy digestion can bother our rest and our sleep.

- **don't eat in front of a digital screen**
  When we don't concentrated on our food, our brains cannot monitor the food we eat. We might eat more quantities than necessary. Let's forget the reruns on TV or our social network for one hour. Let's learn to reprogram our daily way of eating.

- **don't eat too late**
  We should be eating three hours before sleeping. Our body needs time and movement to digest. By eating late, we can have more time for the usual evening activities and naturally burn some calories. If we lie down directly after eating, we might have digestion troubles and a hard time getting to sleep. Let's also avoid to eating junk food before going to bed.

Voilà !

Eating during the three mains meals will help us eat less during the day. If we eat enough, we won't need any extra snacks. That's the best way to teach our body a healthy routine. It sounds quite easy, doesn't it ? We have to check ourselves to find a balance that fits for us and our way of living. No excess, no severe punishments; just a bit of daily attention! Step by step!

Ok, so to start a good habit, let's stand up, take a deep breath, and get a big glass of water!

Habit 2

NO SNACKINGS NO SODAS

Here is one of the secrets of the French and maybe one of the most important to stay healthy: do not drink sugary beverages and not indulge in uncontrolled snacking! I know it might sound harsh, as we all like to grab a chocolate bar and drink sodas from time to time! We have to be aware of our eating habits and find solutions to improve them step by step. Don't worry, I'll give you some tricks and tips to find better alternatives!

TRICKS AND TIPS TO HEALTHY SNACKING

We all know it's hard to resist to a small snack or to wait until lunch or dinner when we are hungry. As we say, we shouldn't stop the habit all at once but step by step. So instead, let's choose healthy snacks. Here is a small list of foods we can use within our menus or keep in hand in case of a sudden snacking desire.

DRINKS

Water

Once again, we have to remember that water has ZERO calories. Water can fill our stomach and help us when we're feeling hungry. We should drink at least 8 glasses a day. Let's get into the habit of drinking a glass of water before our main meals.

Herbal Teas

Herbal teas help us stay calm and feel good.
They are usually very low calorie drinks.

Green Tea

Known for its antioxidant power, green tea helps us in many ways. As a very low calorie drink, it's a natural way to detox and lose weight. We should avoid it from the end of afternoon onwards, because its caffeine might keep us awake at night.

Coffee

Coffee gives us energy and helps us fight tiredness. It can also help us to avoid snacking, but of course we should avoid adding any extra cream and artificial sugars to it!
Similar for teas, it is not recommended to drink coffee at night.

SEASONAL FRUITS AND VEGETABLES

We have to remember to choose seasonal fruits and vegetables.

Apples

Apples are one of the lowest calorie fruits. They have lots of benefits for our health and intestines.

Almonds

Almonds are full of protein and are fiber rich. Their hard texture forces us to bite more. Choose raw almonds and almonds with no extra sugar or dried fruit added, and eat them with moderation.

Lemons

Lemons can be mixed with water and tea.
They provide vitamin C and detox power!

Carrots and Salads

Carrots are water and fiber rich, as well as low in fat. Its texture forces us to take time to bite. You can eat them raw or mixed in green leaf salads with tomatoes: all great snacking! But be sure to avoid lots of dressing!

Pineapples

Pineapples are full of fiber and water.
They are low calorie and help us burn fat.

Bananas

Bananas are full of potassium, magnesium, and vitamins and are perfect afternoon snacking.

Oatmeal

Full of fiber, oatmeal's texture helps us achieve a satisfying feeling of fullness. It's also good mixed with cottage cheese or vegetal milk.

DAIRY PRODUCTS

It's no secret that the French love yogurts, cottage cheeses, cheeses, and butter. France is the biggest dairy producer in the EU. Dairy products are good for one's health by bringing us calcium and protein, but also a moderate amount of fat. French women love yogurt and cottage cheese especially to promote weight management.

Cottage Cheese

Cottage cheese is considered a fresh cheese. It has a soft and creamy texture. Choose the low fat versions, and it will have almost no fat! Full of water, it helps the body hydrate. It contains more protein than yogurt. It is super nutritious and can help you lose weight. Because of its high protein content, it also helps you gain muscle.

Yogurt

Yogurt is made from the bacterial fermentation of milk. It provides protein and calcium, and it may enhance healthy gut bacteria. It may also strengthen our immune system and provide benefits to your digestive health. Once again, avoid adding any artificial flavors and sugar to the yogurt!

But also

Breads

We don't even need to mention here that the French are THE bread addicts! They remain the biggest "baguette" eaters in the world. Nowadays, breads with whole wheat, oats, and cereal grains are becoming more and more popular. Bread will help make you feel full, but be sure to eat it with moderation.

Eggs

Boiled eggs are less than 100 calories.

They provide a lot of protein and little fat.
Eggs are a perfect to start the day.
You can find them sometimes on the counters of French cafés.

Dark Chocolate
This is the one everyone has been waiting for!
Dark chocolate helps reduce stress and feeling hungry.
It's best to eat dark chocolate with moderation .

WHY DO THE FRENCH AVOID SUGARY DRINKS AND SNACKING?

- **Family Education**
  The French are not used to drink sugary drinks and eating junk food at home all day long. Our children's education is rather strict, and parents control what kids eat and drink. Kids are taught from a young age that sugary drinks are not good for their health and will lead to being overweight. The French instead drink a lot of water. In order to avoid snacking, they eat meals 3.5 times a day.

- **Media Information**
  The French are obsessed with their weight and appearance. The French are aware that junk food and bad eating habits can have serious impacts on their health. Also, magazines and media focus regularly on how to stay slim, especially before summer vacations! Tons of studies are often published on how our eating habits affect our health. For example, OECD statistics

show that the obesity rate among French adults are among the lowest of the OECD country members. In the same way, the obesity rate of French kids is not only among the lowest but also hasn't risen much in the last 20 years. If you don't have the time to read general statistics, you just need to type these three words in the search bar of your internet browser: "sugary drink obesity," and check the results.

- **Public Control Authorities**
  The French administration often promotes communication campaigns to push French people to eat well and take care of our health. They released some slogans such as, "Eat 5 fruits and vegetables a day," or, "Eat, move," which is known by everyone in France.

There are also a lot of regulations and laws to protect public health. For example

- sugary drinks and snack vending machines are not allowed in school

- school cafeterias are not allowed to serve sodas but water instead

- school menus are checked and approved by dietitians and administrative authorities

- there is a special tax for purchasing sugary drinks

- restaurants are not allowed to propose free refills of sugary drinks within their menus

Voilà !

Actually, there is no instant and magical formula. Start by learning your daily habits and try to improve them day by day. For example, buy in advance healthy snacks such as yogurt, bananas, and a bottle of water instead of buying junk food and sugary drinks!

Ok, let's stand up, get a piece of paper, and add some healthy snacks to replace cans of sodas with bottled water on our shopping list!

Habit 3

PETIT IS CHIC

One French secret is moderation and not excess. We have to be aware about our way of eating and not eat by habit. The French keep an eye on what they eat everyday.

When you're eating among French people at a restaurant, you'll often hear, "I don't know if I should take dessert," or, "I would like to get this meal, but it's not reasonable." We all know that food in excess will have bad effects on our weight in the long term.

Let's become more aware of our way of eating and not a victim of our hunger!

WHY DO THE FRENCH EAT SMALL PORTIONS?

1. French people are obsessed with their weight

French society used to emphasize appearance and silhouette. During the Middle Ages in Europe, being slim was considered beautiful. Later, the corset, a painful and rigid undergarment became popular among the European kingdom. Being slim has long been a synonym for seduction. In the last century, the development of couture maison and the fashion magazine made this thought even bigger. Though they are among the slimmest in Europe, the French continue to be obsessed with their weight and the will to monitor their weight. In general, French people care about how they look but also want to feel good. That's why they spend a lot of money on their underwear. If you shop in Paris, the number of pastry stores, as well as lingerie stores, might surprise you.

2. Kids way of eating is controlled

The French have a strict education regarding the way to eat. Kids are never left alone to eat. "Help yourself" definitely doesn't exist in French home and schools. Parents control children meals and snacking. In schools, dietitians and French authorities control food. They also learn to eat quantified and sequenced meals. Sugary drinks and snacking vending machines are not allowed inside French schools.

3. French restaurants serve small portions

In French restaurants, every meal is served one after another on an already-portioned plate. Individual portions are smaller compared to some countries. Meat and fish are always served with vegetables or green salads. You can seldom find All You Can Eat restaurants, and doggy bags are not in the French culture. The only thing you can get as a free refill is usually water and sometimes bread.
In the same way, take away food is much smaller than in some countries. The average Paris croissant size might be half the size of the average New York muffin. It's also true for the drinks; you won't find XXL sodas in French fast food.

4. PETIT is CHIC

We should always remember to get food or drinks in moderate quantity and not in excess. In France, the word "petit," which means small, is everywhere: petit dejeuner, petit ami … It is often synonymous of precious or rare: a positive meaning. Even if it is very superficial, the French savoir vivre code is still present in the modern society. Eating small quantities is seen as more educated than eating a huge plate of food like a caveman. Strike the pose!

FRENCH PLAN THEIR FOOD QUANTITY

• Food shopping plan

Planning our food shopping in advance also helps in
planning the quantity of food we will be eating.
It will help us visualize the quantity and the diversity
of our food. It teaches us to become more selective in
our choices of meals and snacking!

• Daily meals plan

The French plan their daily meals in order not to
hungry during the day and be victim of wild snacking.

- ◦ **morning**
  We have to take time to eat so we don't start
  the day with an empty stomach.

- ◦ **lunch**
  Lunch should be the most copious of the day.
  During lunchtime, restaurants usually propose
  different sets with hors d'oeuvre, main dishes,
  and dessert. The French are very gourmet and
  love desserts. We usually want to know what
  kind of dessert is proposed before ordering the
  main dish. Then we can regulate the amount of
  food we'll be eating for lunch.

- ◦ **afternoon**
  We have to plan in advance a healthy snack in
  order not to buy junk food from the nearest
  vending machine.

    ○   **evening**

The French eat a light meal at night. They usually eat salads, soups, or a light dish and light dessert. For long time, the dinner was also called "le souper": dinner made of soup. We avoid all sugar and fatty foods in the evening because they take longer to digest.

• Weekly Meals Plan

Rather than removing a meal during the day, let's learn to eat light after a heavy meal. If we think we will be eating heavier during some special time of the year or some special events, let's plan to eat lighter the week after.

• Don't forget the bread ...

The French have always eaten bread. Bread is part of French food heritage from our agricultural ancestors. Today, the so-called baguette stays the most consumed type of bread in France. Nowadays, the trend of whole wheat breads and cereal breads is growing.
Bread is generally served for free in French restaurants or bistros but without butter or olive oil. It helps us balance our eating and not consume an excess quantity of food. Bread is rich in fiber, complex carbohydrates, and vegetable proteins. We should eat it with moderation.

9 TIPS AND TRICKS TO NOT EAT IN LARGE QUANTITIES

1. Bring a bottle of water on the table before eating.
    Drinking a big glass of water before eating will fill our stomach and deter us from eating large quantities.

2. Prepare meal portions on our plate. This helps us visualize and contain the quantity of food that we will be eating.

3. Cook a large quantity of food in advance but prepare some container to store the excess. We shouldn't keep everything open around the table so we won't be tempted to overeat.

4. Choose reasonably sized plates or bowls and not big ones. This helps us eat normal amounts of food.

5. Eat with a fork and knife rather than a spoon. This will help to divide the food, eat slowly, and lower the amount of food per serving.

6. Cut food into small pieces before putting it inside your mouth. This helps us to visualize the quantity and our portion sizes more accurately.

7. Select healthy snacks in advance: prepare a container of fruit and yogurt for an afternoon snack, and this will save us from running to the nearest vending machine.

8. Avoid sugary drinks and sodas. We shouldn't be drinking our calories but eating them!

9. WE SHOULDN'T BE SNACKING IF WE ARE NOT HUNGRY ANYMORE.
    We have to learn our limit and stop eating junk food by habit.

DO NOT SKIP MEALS IN ORDER TO LOSE WEIGHT.

Everything is always about balance. Losing or gaining weight is about the number of calories we eat and not about the number of meals we eat a day. If we are not hungry before eating breakfast, lunch, or dinner, it is better to eat very light than totally skipping the meal..

As for a quick type of diet, when we skip a meal, our body will use some of its sugar storage but not much fat storage. As a result, during the next meal, our body will use some extra storage again. But our body will remember that it already used this storage before. So to prevent that in the future, it will tend to store a bigger quantity than before. So it might result in excess weight.
And the second piece of bad news is that by skipping a meal, we tend to be hungrier later on. And there is the possibility of snacking on more junk food than expected.

Skipping dinner can have double the consequences as well. When we skip dinner, we might wake up during the night in search of food. Usually, we will choose the easy way to eat, like snacking on junk food. Moreover, we might wake up the next morning tired, with headache, and in bad mood and will to tend to consume extra sugar to feel better.

Voilà !

The good news is that we don't need to follow a severe diet to lose weight. Let's check our daily way of eating and learn to set up some limits step by step. We can find a balanced way of living without excess if we think about it!

Ok, so to celebrate this great news, let's stand up and get a big glass of water!

Habit 4

UN, DEUX, TROIS ...

One of the secrets of the French is to move more often and more naturally as possible. For example, by walking. For the French, physical activity doesn't mean doing sports training. Moving doesn't mean signing up to a gym and getting strict, expensive lessons. The French move everyday in their daily life and create opportunities to move their body.

Come on, let's get started!

WHY DO THE FRENCH WALK A LOT ?

1 - Walking is a french tradition

•	French cities and villages are very condensed, and you can do your shopping most of the time without using a car. There are also a lot of walkways, parks, and gardens inside French cities.

•	The French walk in a family. After long Sunday lunches, French families usually go for a walk together. It's healthy to exercise after a big lunch to help digest. It's also a time where adults walk and talk together, and the kids go and play together.

•	The French consider walking as an activity. They like to walk during their vacations. There are a lot of walking camps, and hiking is very popular.

2 - Walking has a lot of advantages

○	almost everyone can do it

○	we don't need any special gear

○	we can walk anywhere

○	we can walk alone or with other people

8 TIPS
TO WALK MORE OFTEN

1
let's walk to do our daily shopping

2
when we use public transportation, let's get off
one station before or after where our job is located
so we can add some distance to walk

3
when we use a car,
let's park a little farther from our destination

4
when we go to the supermarket,
let's not park close to the main entrance

5
let's pick up the kids from school by walking;
that way our kids will also learn to walk more often

6
let's walk with friends in the city while shopping
or trekking during the weekend

7
let's walk longer distances with our pet
8
let's plan ahead and bring walking shoes in our bag
when we go to work so we can have business shoes and
walking shoes

TIPS AND TRICKS TO MOVE MORE OFTEN NATURALLY EVERYDAY

• Set up some Smartphone Alarms

Our way of living has become more and more static. We tend to move less and less. We sometimes even have three screens in front of us at the same time. Our whole body, from head, neck, back, and legs become inactive. Let's program some alarms on our smartphones to remind us that we have to move every two hours, for example. There are plenty of applications that we can find to force us to move more everyday. Why don't we move while chatting on social networks or calling a friend? Let's stand up instead of lying down for hours!

• Stairs

Let's use stairs more often instead of the elevator. We can use the steps to exercise at our own pace every time we use stairs. Taking the stairs is good for the heart, hips and legs. Whether at home, shopping malls, the office, or school, let's take the chance to use stairs instead of the elevator.

• Let's Move at Home

Let's play some music, stand up, and move a bit. We can also move more energetically or dance while we do domestic tasks.

For example:

- cleaning

- ironing

- playing with kids

- playing with pets

• Solo Core Training

When we use public transportation, we can think about our abdomen and practice core training. Let's contract our abdomen muscles and then relax them. Let's do that while breathing deeply. We can also practice this kind of exercise while we sit in front of our computer.

• Breath Deeply

Every time we move or exercise, we shouldn't neglect the process of breathing deeply. Deep breathing has many benefits. It helps us move our body and bring oxygen all over our body. Meditation and being focused on our breathing before sleeping will help us digest food better and sleep well.

WHY DO WE HAVE TO MOVE?

We'd need another book to explain how sports and moving our body benefits our health. First of all, internally we are always in motion and never stop: we breathe, we digest, our blood moves, etc. Moving our body helps our cells receive oxygen. It helps our body produce natural hormones, such as dopamine to boost our brain, serotonin to get rid of stress, or melatonin to help our sleep.

That's why we should have dynamic physical activity at least 30 minutes a day. It doesn't help to do it once and then do nothing for the rest of the week. We have to teach ourselves to get into a daily routine that we can commit to for a long-term basis.

So, let's move!

MOVE ESPECIALLY DURING A DIET

Being on a diet doesn't mean we don't need to move and need physical activity. When we are on a diet, we tend to reduce our incoming energy. Our body will react and try to get the extra energy it needs from our muscles. When we will go back to eating normally again, we will eat in bigger quantities. So our body will transform this excess energy into fat. That's why we have to maintain our muscles mass in our body. By having regular physical activity, we can eliminate these excess calories after you're finished dieting.

WHAT TO EAT BEFORE AND AFTER PHYSICAL ACTIVITY ?

- ## Before Exercising

It's not recommended to exercise without eating anything. We should eat at least two and a half hours before doing physical activities. It's better to eat slow-release carbs. Before exercise, let's have fruit or a sugary drink and of course a lot of water!
This is dependent on the activity; of course our goal is not to push you to drink sodas before using the stairs to reach the next floor!

- ## After Exercising

We should be drinking a lot of water. Let's rehydrate our body!
One hour after exercising, we can eat again. Better avoid foods that are high in fat and sugar at this time, as our body will tend to store them. Let's eat foods that are heavy in proteins and keep the meal light if it's dinner time.

LET'S GET MOTIVATION IN ORDER TO MOVE

Before being able to move every day, we have to get out of our daily, safe routine. We have to be motivated! With a bit of organization and scheduling, we can start to move more and more everyday without even thinking about it!

Let's set up goals for our health and our well being; we'll gradually gain daily good habits!

Voilà !

Finally, all of this is about making the right habits step-by-step and everyday. Let's analyze our present condition and daily routine. Let's think about all the opportunities we have to move our body instead of sitting or lying down. Let's plan this in our daily and weekly schedule! After all, it is all about feeling better!

Ok, let's stand up, drink a big glass of water, and walk around the neighborhood for a while!

Habit 5

BALANCE AND VARIETY

One French secret is to balance and diversify what we eat. For the French, eating well means eating a large variety of foods.

France has geographic variety and has 4 seasons. We can find all kind of landscapes in France: fields, mountains, lakes, seas, forest, greens… It has been an agricultural country for centuries. That's why we have such a diversity in our animal and vegetable production in those area. There are a lot of products from individual territories, like, for example, more than 300 different cheese. That's why French people learn to eat a variety of foods based on the area they live and the season.

The good news is that the French don't really have forbidden foods or miracle treatments. It's all about balance and what we eat daily and weekly. Let's be free to eat what we want, but be responsible!

HOW DO THE FRENCH BALANCE THEIR MEALS?

We know that our body has multiple needs, such as fat, sodium, minerals, vitamins, iron... We have to find a way to provide all these elements to avoid deficiency and excess. That's why we think we have to eat a variety of food during our different meals to satisfy those natural needs.

Here are some rules the French have to balance their meals:

Breakfast « Le Petit Déjeuner »

- hot drink (tea, coffee, chocolate)

- cereal product (bread, cereals, corn flakes)

- dairy product (milk, cheese, yogurt)

- fruit or fruit juice (with no added sugar)

- balanced foods for hungrier people

Lunch « Le Déjeuner »

- raw vegetables or green salad

- protein portion: meat, fish or eggs

- cooked vegetables (no fried food everyday)

- dairy products (milk, cheese, yogurt)

- starchy foods: rice, pasta, potatoes, dry vegetables,

- cereals or bread

- fruit

Afternoon snacking « Le 4 heures »

While not always necessary for adults, growing kids should have cereal, dairy products, and fruits.

Dinner « Le diner »

Usually, it's a light version of lunch. For example: main dish, green salad, dessert.
We should always keep the main foods balanced with such items as proteins, raw or cooked vegetables, dairy products, bread, and dessert. Choose foods that makes you sleepy, such as: starchy foods, dairy products, and bananas.

Kids School

Menus in French schools are created by dietitians and controlled by the French administration. Menus are scheduled in advance - usually monthly so they can have various food types among the main dish, vegetables, dairy products, and desserts. Parents can also check the menu on internet.

Kids menus are diversified and should include:

- hors d'oeuvre : vegetables or salads

- main dish : meat, fish, or eggs served with cooked vegetables

- dessert : yogurt, fruits, cake, or starchy foods

HOW DO THE FRENCH DIVERSIFY FOOD?

- **Eating 5 fruits and vegetables a day**
  We have to condition ourselves to eat fruits and
  vegetables every day. French kids learn that eating
  fruits and vegetables is good for their health. Fruits
  and vegetables are essential in our daily food because
  they are naturally rich in vitamins, minerals,
  antioxidants, fibers and low in fat and calories.
  They bring a lot of water to our body. For example,
  here are some of the most water-filled vegetables and
  fruits: cucumber, tomatoes, salads, lettuce, pumpkin,
  melon, strawberry, apple, orange, lemon, carrots,

  Each of our meals should contains 2/3 vegetable
  dishes, such as vegetables, rice, cereals, pasta, and whole rice.

- **Eating seasonal fruits and vegetables**
  Fruits and vegetables grow best in suitable weather
  conditions for them. They give us the right nutritions
  when they are grown at the right time of the year.
  Seasonal fruits and vegetables naturally contain more
  vitamins, minerals, and antioxidants. Moreover, they
  will be picked at the right time and will have the best
  flavor.
  In the winter time, cold and lack of sun affects us
  more. Our body needs more energy to warm up.
  That's why we should eat more vegetables like
  cabbage, lettuce, sweet potatoes, and pumpkin.
  In the summer time, the heat and sun are stronger. Our
  body needs more water. We can choose seasonal fruits
  and vegetables such as watermelon, melons,
  strawberry, and tomatoes to fill that void.
  Sometimes, fruits and vegetables sold in supermarkets

are not always seasonal products. They are grown far from the place of consumption. So they are usually grown with a lot of artificial products to keep the same shape and color in order please the city consumers all year long. We have to slow down this type of consumption and try to get more real and seasonal products.

By matching our food to our seasonal needs, we also vary the taste of our food all year long.

• Organic Food

Organic food is not only a fashion trend for hipsters. In France, organic agriculture is more and more present and keeps growing. It has to follow specific laws to regulate animal and vegetable production.

Organic agriculture emphasizes local and seasonal production with respect to nature. Following the trend, we can see now a lot of organic stores and chains on the market.

They propose more and more diversified products and provide new choices for consumers of vegan and gluten free foods.

• Dairy Products

France is one of the biggest dairy producers and consumers inside the EU. The have large productions, and the products range from: cheese, butter, cream, yogurt … Dairy products have calcium, protein, and energy. The French are among the biggest consumers of cheese in the world. Generally, women prefer cottage cheese and yogurt because some cheese can be seen as fat products.

- ## Spices, Roots, Seeds and Vegetable Oils

  Let's use more of those all natural resources instead of industrial seasonings. Spice, root, seed, and vegetable oils can improve the flavor of our meals and bring us more iron and minerals.

  A lot of ancient cultures such as Chinese and Indian consider food as medicine. The deep knowledge of these natural resources can lead us toward better health. They can even help us to heal some physical and mental conditions. We have to consider food as something very positive for health and vary our ingredients regarding :

  - sugary / salty

  - fat / non-fat

  - raw / cooked

  - acid / basic

  - alcohol / non alcohol

  - vegetable / animal

  - fried / boiled

  - liquid / solid

2 FRENCH TIPS TO VARY FOOD

1 - ADAPT our current menus regarding our general consumption

We must adapt our meals regarding planned excesses.
For example, when we know that we will have a big dinner
planned, let's eat less during lunch or the day after. Especially
during end of the year, we always have a lot of family gatherings
and big meals planned. So in this case, we will balance the first
week of January by eating lighter - more fruits and vegetables. This
way we can achieve an average balance all year long.

2 - PLAN our food variety

We should plan our food variety weekly so that

- we can plan a diversified menu

- we avoid making quick decision to choose easy snacking

- we can plan our organization and preparation
  of the meal

- we avoid wasting food

DON'T EAT (IN EXCESS)

Fried Food
We must limit our fried food consumption.
We have to realize that most fast food or take away food
is mainly fried food like: potatoes, chicken, and fish.
Unfortunately, when foods are fried, they lose most of their
vitamins and nutrients. Under the high temperature of fried
cooking, the bad oil fats will replace the water of the original
components. Also, let's remember that excessive consumption of
fried foods can create heart and weight issues.

Sodas
If we want to lose weight quickly,
we should first stop drinking a lot of unneeded calories.
The calories we need should come from eating not drinking.

Junk Food
We may have the bad habit of buying junk food from shops.
Why don't we instead choose some healthy snacks?
We can avoid eating:
- processed fat
- artificially added sugars
- sugary drinks

Voilà !

It's less difficult than it seems. Let's try to balance and diversify our food everyday. In order to get extra motivation, let's think of the important different food and meals, how it makes us healthier, and also adds to our social network stories!!!

Habit 6

DRINKING WATER

Don't look for magic potions or any other miraculous drink anymore! The good news is that one of the main French secrets to staying healthy is to drink... water ! Yes, you heard that correctly! We should remember that water is the only drink without added sugar and calories. It's also the only drink essential to our body.

So let's learn to make water our best friend!

WHY DO FRENCH PEOPLE DRINK MAINLY WATER?

France has lots of natural water sources, and it rains a lot most of the year. In the past, French cities were built close to water. Today, potable water is available in every house in France. There is a lot of it, and it is very cheap. That's why at home, kids are taught to drink water and to avoid sugary drinks for health and economic reasons.

When we go to restaurants in France, we can choose flat water called "eau du robinet" which is free and comes with free refills. Otherwise, we can pay and choose bottled mineral water called "eau plate."

Due to the country's great natural resources, France became the first mineral water exporter in the world. A lot of famous brands are manufactured in the country, such as Evian, Vittel, and Volvic. French people usually carry a small bottle of water everyday in their bag. They are among the biggest bottled water consumers in Europe.

WHAT ARE OTHER FAVORITE DRINKS IN FRANCE?

- **Sparkling Water**

If we are addicted to small bubbles, sparkling water can be the perfect substitute for sugary drinks.
Sparkling water contains CO_2. This gas can have multiple origins. It can be of natural volcanic origin, or it can be artificial. In both cases, the effects are about the same, as we drink CO_2 anyway.
Sparkling water is sometimes recommended to help digestion.
Some drinks are also rich in calcium and magnesium.

Sparkling water is not recommended for:
- people who suffer from aerophagia, as it will encourage symptoms
- people who have a low sodium diet or have high blood pressure, as some types of carbonated beverages contain sodium.

•   Tea

Tea is the second most consumed drink in the world behind water.
It can be served in many flavors and can be drunk cold or hot. Tea
can contain teine, which comes from the tea leaves.
There are lots of tea varieties, and each of them has specific
benefits, such as: helping with digestion, detoxing, and relaxing.
For example, green tea has a lots of health benefits, such as
antioxidants, and it may protect the brain from aging.
Tea is a rich source of tannins, known for reducing iron absorption.
This is not advised for people with low iron or pregnant women.

•   Coffee

The French usually drink black coffee in the morning and espressos
at the end of the meal or anytime during the day. Coffee can be
good for our body if we don't over-drink it. Of course, we should
avoid drinking coffee before sleeping. It's been shown to provide
antioxidant activity as well. It can boost our energy for a while and
make us feel good.

•   Decaffeinated Coffee

Decaffeinated coffee is called "deca" in France. It is very useful for
those who are addicted to coffee! We can drink it more often than
regular coffee because of its lack of caffeine. Sometimes the
fabrication of decaffeinated coffee uses chemical substances, so we
should drink it with moderation.

•   Chicory

Well-known for its digestion benefits, chicory is one of the few
drinks made from roots. It is fiber and mineral rich, with very few
calories and no caffeine. It can be good natural substitute for coffee.

- ### Herbal Teas

Herbal teas, also called "tisanes" or "infusions" are very popular among French people.

French women love them and have herbal tea often, especially after heavy meals or before sleeping.

There are many kinds of herbal teas, and each of them has specific benefits.

We can prepare herbal teas the traditional way by pouring hot water over it the leaves. Nowadays, it is very easy to find them in every supermarket. They come in small packages in the same shape as tea bag.

8 popular herbs used in herbal teas

1. **Lavender :**
   lavender herbal tea helps relax the body, promote healthy digestion, and aids in falling asleep
   (best to drink before sleeping)

2. **Verbena :**
   verbena herbal tea helps promote healthy digestion and aids in falling asleep
   (best to drink after meals and before sleeping)

3. **Chamomile :**
    chamomile herbal tea helps promote sleep and reduces
    insomnia, boosts immunity, and treats colds, but it is not
    recommended for children or people who have allergies,
    especially to pollens
    (best to drink after meals and before sleeping)

4. **Linden tree :**
    linden tree herbal tea calms anxiety, helps fight inflammation,
    and promotes sleeping
    (best to drink after meals and before sleeping)

5. **Ginger:**
    this root originated from China and has powerful medicinal
    properties, such as lowering blood sugar and improving heart
    disease risk factors
    (best to drink the morning)

6. **Thyme :**
    thyme herbal tea helps lower blood pressure, boosts immunity,
    disinfects, and helps boost your mood
    (best to drink in the morning and can be a substitute for
    morning coffee)

7. **Mint :**
    mint herbal tea helps you feel more awake, helps digestion, and
    boosts liver and stomach function
    (best to drink in the morning or after lunch)

8. **Ginseng :**
    this root is well known by Chinese medicine; ginseng boosts the
    immune system and fight tiredness and increases energy levels
    (best to drink in the morning)

HOW ABOUT SUGARY DRINKS?

French people have thought for a long time that drinking sugary drinks and sodas is bad for our health. Kids are usually not allowed to drink it at home or at school. For those who are addicted to sodas and don't drink water, please search the internet using three words: sugary drink obesity. There are a lot of surveys related to body disorders and being overweight due to over consumption of sugary drinks.

Ok, so now, let's explain a bit why water is essential to our health.

WHY DO WE HAVE TO DRINK WATER?

Water is one of the three essential elements that we need to survive. The two other elements are oxygen to breathe and food to eat. We usually say that we can survive three minutes without breathing, three days without drinking, and 30 days without eating.

The 5 main functions of water are:

1. **Feed our body oxygen (the blood)**
   The human body is made of 60% water. The bloody liquid called plasma is made up 90% of water. Blood helps circulate oxygen in our body. Cells, organs, and muscles absorb oxygen and then reject CO2. That's one reason why water is essential to our body.

2. **Eat and digest (the saliva)**
   Saliva is 99% water. Saliva helps food move and digest. Without water, there is no saliva, and then no digestion possible. Water makes digestion fluid and helps prevent issues with constipation.

3. Eliminate waste (the urine)

Urine is 95% water. With the help of our kidneys, urine helps eliminate and evacuate waste and the body's toxins. This process helps keep the minerals brought by water.

4. Regulate our temperature (the sweat)

For an adult, body temperature can be anywhere from 97 F to 99 F. Fevers and sweating uses water to help our body control its temperature. The hotter the weather is, the more we should drink water in order to hydrate our body.

5. Protect our body (the skin)

Our skin is mainly made of water. Water helps skin cells regenerate. Skin protects us against outside aggressions such as cold, the sun, microbes, and etc. Dry or neglected skin gets older faster and is unable to protect us as well.

HOW MUCH WATER SHOULD WE DRINK EVERYDAY?

A typical adult size loses 2.5 liters of water a day with urine, breathing, and sweat. We need to replace this water by drinking. We get water from food, fruits, vegetables, coffee, tea, and soup.

We should be drinking a minimum of eight glasses of water a day. This is the so-called 8X8 rule. If we live in high temperature areas, when we exercise, and when we are sick or have diarrhea, we lose more water than usual, so we should even drink more.

To help us drink our daily dose of water, we can prepare some water in a bottle every morning to remind us visually that we need to drink water everyday.

WHEN SHOULD WE DRINK WATER?

Often! Excessive consumption of water isn't a health danger. But if we tend to drink more than 16 glasses a day, it's a good idea to see a doctor and check that we don't have any hormonal disorders or diabetes. We have to drink in order to avoid dehydration. Lack of water can result in dark urine, dry skin, and a dry throat.

We should be drinking water regularly all day long and not waiting until we're thirsty to drink. It is better to drink small quantities of water throughout the day and not huge amounts at once. It is recommended to drink a glass of water when we wake up. Drinking water or herbal teas before sleeping helps combat dehydration. But we shouldn't drink a lot before sleeping if we don't want to wake up in the middle of the night to go to the restroom.

To remind us that we need to drink, let's set some alarms on our smartphones, for example, every two hours. So from now on, don't forget to leave the house every morning with a bottle of water!

Voilà !

To conclude, we don't need to be Nobel prize winner to realize that water is essential to our body and our good health. We should keep in mind that in every industrialized country, we have access to unlimited drinking water! We should stop complaining and enjoy these simple things as much as we can!

OK, so to celebrate this good news, let's stand up, take a deep breath, and drink a big glass of water!!!

Habit 7

SLOW LIFE

One of the secrets of the French is to eat slowly. Life is short, so take time to enjoy life and savor everything you eat!

We live in a society where everything is getting faster and faster: work, information, transportation, communication…. We tend to automate our eating to reduce lunchtime and optimize our daily schedule. But we have to realize that our body has a natural rhythm that is slower than our stressed daily lifestyle. Our way of eating should not be overlooked, which could lead to more diseases.

Let's slow down!

WHY DO THE FRENCH TAKE TIME TO EAT?

• Savor what we eat

We have to appreciate what we eat: taste, color, layout.... The French are gourmets, and to eat means to please ourselves.

• Enjoy present time

Eating is not only the act of swallowing food and drink. It's a special moment to relax. We should appreciate this time and turn this usual act into happiness. The French love to talk and exchange ideas and feelings. Eating or drinking are perfect moments to be shared.

• Thank your host

We all know that cooking requires time. When someone is cooking for us, we should appreciate the time and effort this person took. Taking time and appreciating food is a way to thank and respect our host.

The French restaurant service requires time
When we go to restaurants in France, we shouldn't expect to be seated or served quickly. Waiters are usually very few and very busy. As French service takes time due to the sequence of the meal, lunch can easily take one hour. The waiter has to come to take different orders, such as drink, meals, desserts, and coffee and then they must bring out each meal. All of this determines how much time lunch takes, which is definitely not fast food.

WHY EATING SLOWLY
MAY REDUCE WEIGHT GAIN ?

We all tend to eat fast in order to go back to our previous tasks. But we should know that eating fast might lead to gaining weight.

We should concentrate on what we are eating because our brain plays a big role in our digestion process. First, our brain will send messages to our salivary glands during the meal. Saliva is essential to our digestion and to our taste perception. We all know how the smell of a barbecue or the sight of a chocolate macaron can stimulate our appetite and produce saliva. They can make our mouths water! Then, we have to remember that our brain needs 20 minutes to understand that we've eaten enough.

When we eat too fast, our brain doesn't have time to understand that we've eaten enough. So we stay hungry and tend to eat more food than necessary, which might lead us to more snacking. And guess what? We may gain more weight!

So let's try to eat lunch slower in order to avoid wild snacking in the afternoon.

WHY IS CHEWING
GOOD FOR YOUR HEALTH?

When we eat fast, we tend to swallow quickly instead of chewing our food. We should bite and chew our food many times if we want to avoid gas, stomachaches, and digestion troubles.

Why do we have to chew that long?

Chewing is an essential part of digestion.

- Saliva enzymes will start to set some glucose free, which will tend to make us feel more satisfied with the food

- Chewing helps stomach digestion work. When we send food that is not chewed properly into our stomach, it can force the stomach to work extra hard, which might result in acid reflux

- Chewing makes our gums and jaw stronger

- Chewing forces our face muscles to work and helps them to stay firm and young

- Chewing helps us spend more time eating slowly

10 TIPS TO EAT SLOWER

1. Choose food that needs to be chewed and not drank

2. Cut our meals in small pieces

3. Eat smaller portions so we can take time to savor our food

4. Chew the food longer in our mouth

5. Put back your fork, knife, chopstick or spoon on the table between every bite

6. In the same style, put back your sandwich or finger-food on the table between every bite

7. Eat with chopsticks, even if we are not used to

8. Eat with your hands, even if we are not used to

9. Prepare more frequently our meals by ourselves. In this way, we'll take more time to enjoy the time we spent preparing our meal

10. Eat first with your eyes. We live in a society where image is more important than ever. Take more time to look at your plate before putting everything in your mouth.
    Savor with your eyes first before eating.

FOOD MEDITATION
For those who really want to take their time,
be aware about the present moment and concentrate on
texture, color, smell, and presentation of the food.
We'll increase our happiness while eating.

THE DIGESTION PROCESS IS NATURALLY LONG

Our body works in a different rhythm than our lifestyle. Usually, the digestion process needs time to work well. It has several steps, which naturally take time. The whole cycle of food transformation takes about 24 hours from the time the food is in our mouth until we get rid of the residues.

First, we put the food into the mouth. Food is bitten and chewed with the teeth. Then saliva will transform the food with natural enzymes. Then it will be sent to the stomach through esophagus. The stomach will knead the food with the gastric juices until it becomes the consistency of porridge.
This step takes 3 to 4 hours.

The food then will move into the small intestine, which will select and keep beneficial nutrients. This step takes 6 to 7 hours.

The leftover will move then into the colon before reaching the rectum before being evacuated.
This step also takes 6 to 7 hours.

So let's be aware of our natural rhythm in order to adapt to it our life rhythm.

TAKE TIME AFTER MEALS

We shouldn't do anything for at least 15 minutes after finishing meals. This helps our body start the digestion process. We should move a bit but not engage in any heavy exercise. If you're at home, you can clean the table, kitchen, and dishes.

Right after a meal, we shouldn't:

- **Chew gum**
  Chewing gum can be good for our breath, but it can bring air into your stomach. It can disturb your digestion and also create some undesirable gas and stomachaches.

- **Lie down**
  Lying down right after a meal will upset the digestion process. Food moves harder into the body, and this may slow down digestion. It can also make gastric liquid come up and create burning sensations. So let's wait a while after a meal before taking a nap!

- **Sit down**
  Sitting all day long might bother the digestion process, especially if we don't sit in the right position. Take a small walk before going back to sit in front of your computer.

- **Partake in sports or working out**
  During digestion, our body sends oxygenated blood into our stomach. When we are doing sports, our body needs to send blood into our muscles. So if we do both at the same time, our brain needs to make choice, which will not be good for our health and our digestion.

Voilà !

Pausing to eat is part of our daily happiness. To enjoy it, we must slow down our life rhythm during meals. Life is short, so let's try to increase our happiness!

So let's stop to running everywhere. Let's take a deep breath and then let's get a big glass of water. Meanwhile, let's think about what we will eat for the next meal!

Habit 8

HOME MADE COOKING

One of the secrets of the French is the "fait maison," which literally means in French, "home made." The French have cooked for centuries at home. They developed a lifestyle around the house, the family, and home cooking.

So let's check it out more in detail.

WHY DO THE FRENCH TEND TO COOK AT HOME? ?

• **Family transmission of knowledge**

France has been mainly an agricultural country for centuries. The French were living in the rhythm of the seasons in a rural mode. Everyone created their own recipes with the local products. Recipes were passed down through generations.

• **Rural heritage**

For a long time, France was mainly a rural country. Social life was very local and among family houses in the area. Even if nowadays urbanization is becoming more massive, there are still a lot of villages where there is no fast food, no shopping malls, but just food shops. French people eat inside the house rather than outside. So they still cook a lot at home. In the same way, they enjoy having parties at their houses and inviting friends to their home rather than gathering everyone at a restaurant. French families eat together in restaurants only for special occasions.

• **Le potager**

Before the development of the big cities, the French lived most of the time inside houses rather than in apartments. Most of them had a garden. It was very common to use part of this garden to grow some fruits, vegetables, and even have a chicken or a rabbit. This was called "le potager," which means "kitchen garden," but it is also the place where vegetable soup (also called "le potage") comes from. The most popular vegetables are: carrots, lettuce, tomatoes, radishes, potatoes, and fruits like apples, cherries, strawberries, and raspberries. The products they cooked came directly from the garden, so from the producer directly, and the production was 100% local and equitable!

THE FRENCH LOVE BUYING FOOD AT SMALL STORES AND MARKETS

French love craft stores and independent businesses. Moreover, shopping at these stores develops human links and better a social life. There is a tradition for this kind of shopping in France and in Europe. In every village, the minimum shops we can still find are bakeries, pastry shops, and vegetables and fruit shops.

In the middle of the 20th century, supermarkets started to expand and kill these small stores. But recently, the trend of quality foods and having human links has become popular again, and we can see a new generation of independent and specialized stores opening again.

In France, we can still easily find small store such as:

- « **la boulangerie** » for the breads

- « **la pâtisserie** » for the cakes

- « **la boucherie** » for the meats

- « **le traiteur** » for prepared food

- « **la poissonnerie** » for sea products

- « **le maraicher** » for fruits and vegetables

We can also find those independent products in the market. You can find "marché" everywhere in France. There are several different merchants, and the products change depending on the location and the season. To go shopping to the marche is a real activity for French people. The French love going shopping there, as we can take time checking the different stands, and we can talk with the sellers and meet some acquaintances.

Let's try to shop more often to the independent merchants and save our local ecosystem!

8 HOMEMADE COOKING BENEFITS

1. Rediscovering food's real taste

In industrial food, flavors are artificial and contain too much salt, sugar, and other added products. By cooking at home, we will need to change our shopping habits and buy real, unprocessed products. Then we'll start to rediscover the real flavor of food. We know our homemade salads are the best in the world!

2. Product selection

By cooking at home, we can choose products that suite our needs, moods, planned menus, and the season. But also keep in mind all those food disease scandals, such as the mad cow and avian influenza. By being selective with our food shopping, we can choose local producers and have a clearer vision about what we are going to eat!

3. Waste control

When we buy fruits, vegetables, meat, and fish to prepare our meals, it's easier to conserve them if we don't use all of it at once. We can recycle leftovers into soup, gratins, and cakes. When we buy industrially processed foods or meals such as pizzas and fast food meals, we all know it's very hard to keep them fresh and impossible to recycle them. And usually we'll have a bad reflex to eat the whole meal, even when we are no longer hungry. And guess what is gonna happen… we might gain weight!

4. Cooking without frying

When they cook at home, french seldom use frying cooking , the cooking of food in fat or oils. To prepare meals, They boiled a lot with water and use the oven to bake. French dont eat french fries everyday even if they are so called !

5. Creating seasoning

The French using very few artificial dressings in their meals. Instead, they make their own dressings, even mustard or mayonnaise. Most often, they use vinegar, salt, pepper, and olive oil to put on top of salad. We also use spices, cream, and vegetable oil to create our own sauces.

6. Creating drinks

We can also be creative to make our own drinks at home. We can add lemon or ginger into water. We can mix herbs and create our own herbal teas. Nowadays, with cheaper kitchen appliances, we can also become a detox juice master by mixing healthy fruits, vegetables, and herbs such as: lemon, honey, mint, cucumber, spinach, apple, carrot, ginger, and cucumber.

7. Personal Satisfaction

What a joy and pride to be able to serve a homemade meal to the one we love! We can find more self-confidence and self-esteem by doing that. And to be honest, it's feels much better to post our finished products on social networks rather than the cheap sandwich we bought at the nearest fast food restaurant!

8. Spending less money

France has a strong agricultural production. We can buy fruits, vegetables, and meat that is not too expensive and is also good quality.

It's usually cheaper to buy raw food and prepare it at home rather than eating out everyday. Also, by doing so, we use fewer paper boxes and plastic containers. We develop local economy and save our money and our planet!

INDUSTRIAL FOOD DISADVANTAGES

Artificial processed food

Industrial food claims to make our life easier, but how about our health? We need to be aware about those processes and improvements in the quality of our daily food.
If we look closer at the label on the frozen products that we usually find in the supermarket, we can discover lists of ingredients that we've never heard of. Most of the natural ingredients don't exist anymore. Instead, we find lists of:

- **colorings** to give a natural color to processed food

- **artificial flavors** to make those products more attractive

- **preservatives** so the products can be kept longer

- **texture additives** to look like a real product

Fast food

Have we ever noticed that most all fast food is soft? All processed food has a soft texture so we can eat more of it faster. We don't need to chew anymore, and we tend to swallow everything like ducks. So what's gonna happen one hour after eating this kind of food? Most of the time we will still be hungry. So we might want to eat again and spend double the money!
Can't we stop and think a bit more?

Pollution

All these processed food industries create a lot of pollution. There is more and more garbage due to the expansion of merchandising goods and packaging. Plastic bags keep feeding into ocean currents, killing tons of sea animals. Industrial agriculture uses too many chemicals and creates ground pollution.

Added sugar dependency

Can we become addicted to sugar?

Dopamine is a chemical substance freed by our brain that associated with pleasurable sensations, particularly when we consume artificial substances such as drugs, but also sugar. That's why it is often called the "feel good" hormone. When the award system is working, we can create actions we want to repeat until it becomes an addiction. Foods that have a lot of fat and sugar have a high glycemic index. Those foods will provide a rush of sugar, and the brain will release dopamine.

So it's actually easy to become addicted to sugar and ... processed food and ... artificial snackings and ... sugar added drinks ...

That's why we have to check our food daily and ensure quality of our snacks!

Why are we attracted to sugar?

Some explanations say that sugar attraction is the result of natural evolution of the human race. In nature, sugar indicates a presence of glucose, which is an energy source for humans.
Some flowers will produce sweet fragrances to attract insects in order to spread pollen and help the survival of their species.
Acidic flavors are often a synonym of toxins or poisons in nature. We've all seen cats and dogs eating grass to help them throw up or clean their own stomach.
So in order to survive as a species and get enough energy to live, our instincts lead us toward sugary foods.

Once again, that's why we have to check
our food daily and ensure quality of our snacks!

Voilà !

It's easy to understand that home cooking pushes us to pay more attention to our food and so to our health. We don't need to be a three-star chef to cook a vegetable dish or prepare a salad.

So, from now on, let's save money, buy some fresh vegetables and some olive oil, and prepare a healthy buddha bowl at home!

Habit 9

A TABLE

One French secret is that French people consider eating as a real activity. To them, eating is not only the act of swallowing food and drink. It's a social activity that they can enjoy and, if possible, share.

WHAT'S THE FRENCH TRADITION?

For the French, eating is a real activity. In France, time to eat is not only a time to satisfy our hunger. It is not something we do while driving, working, or watching TV. Eating requires special time in their daily schedule.

Meals are also moments of social sharing where we talk and exchange ideas among family, friends or colleagues. In France, during a workday lunch time, eating with colleagues or friends is usual. It's not a moment where everyone is running around eating fast food alone or doing something else and eating at the same time. We usually take at least a one hour lunch break.

Among friends, the French don't go out only to have drink. We usually have a drink first and then eat together. Even when teenagers meet in fast food or cheap restaurants, it's more to meet each other and spend time together than buying take away or drive in.

4 FRENCH EATING AND DRINKING HABITS

Except daily meals, there are special moments where French people like to gather and share happy times together eating and drinking.

1. L'Apéritif

« L'apéritif » or « l'apero » This is an old tradition which originated around the Mediterranean sea in Ancient Greece and Egypt. It was the pre-dinner or pre-lunch drink to get yourself hungry before eating.
Nowadays, it's a time of leisure and conviviality to celebrate happy events or the end of the day. Every event is an excuse to spend time to have a drink together.
The French spend this moment at home, at cafes, or at bars usually after work or before eating.
At home with guests, before eating, the French generally start by having a first drink of alcohol together with amuse bouche, which are small starters. It's a sequence before the meal and can

be taken in a different room other than the dining room.
Aperitifs Habits are different around the areas of France. For example, we'll drink more alcohol like Pastis or Rosé in south France, cider in west France and Bretagne, and beer in northern and eastern France. But there are no rules and everybody drinks whatever they feel like.
Champagne is usually reserved for special occasions like birthdays, special family events, or professional events.
For kids also, « l'aperitif » is a special moment. Following this ritual, they have the right to drink something else other than water - for instance juice or sodas! Yeah! Party time!

2. Marathon Lunch

During special family meetings or important social life events such as religious events, weddings, and newborn baby celebrations, the French have the tradition where people gather and have meals that can lasts hours. They don't spend hours eating, but the table is a place to gather around and spend time talking and sharing time together.

3. Digestifs and Pousse Cafe

The so-called « digestif » literally means something that helps digestion. Actually, it is a strong alcohol (usually about 40° alcohol by liter) like Cognac, Armagnac, or whisky that French people drink at the end of a meal.

Le « pousse-café » literally means « to push coffee ». It is the famous digestif that the French like to drink at the end of lunch or dinner after the dessert and the coffee. Strong alcohol is supposed to burn the fat that they have just consumed from the meal and make it easier to digest. The real meaning is to spend more time together and finish with happy times sharing strong alcohol.

Until last century, during this long family meals, this kind of strong alcohol drink was even served between different courses during a meal. People thought that drinking strong alcohol between courses would help them digest the previous dish so they could eat more.
In Normandie, the so-called « trou normand » (Normandie cut) drinks between meals, was made from strong apple alcohol called Calvados. Nowadays, with the French administration has become more and more severe with alcohol consumption, so this kind of habit has started to disappear.

4. Le Café

Drinking coffee is typically another social act in France. It is not only the act of getting a latte at the closest take away.
When French people propose to have a coffee, it's to have a friendly and informal break and to spend some informal time together to talk rather than just buying a latte at the nearest take away.
« Le café » is also the name for a public space. It is the most important social place in France where everyone can spend time regardless of their social class, gender, or age. Friends, couples, and colleagues meet each other to spend and share some time drinking. It's a place where you can spend time standing up at the counter or sit. The French love to spend time sitting on the terrasse and talking while watching the people walking around.

HOW DO FRENCH KIDS LEARN TO EAT ?

- ## A Table

The French think that eating is a social activity that has to be taught to kids. From their young age, French kids get a strict education about eating. It's the opposite of the « help yourself. » Kids learn to eat with other people and not alone in their bedroom or in front of a smartphone. They also have to learn good eating habits and manners.

Within the family, meals are eaten at the same time, and it is a life routine. Usually, the adult of the family prepares the meals. When it's time to eat, they will call the whole family to announce that dinner is ready. But the significance is a bit different. We say « A TABLE » which literally means: come to the table. The meaning is: please come and join everybody around the table so we can start eating together. It doesn't mean dinner is ready so take it and eat it whenever and wherever you want.

- ## Dish Sequence

In France, during lunch and dinner, meals are sequenced and everyone follows this ritual. First, we eat the hors d'oeuvre, then the main dish, then green salad in option, followed by cheese or dairy product, and finally dessert.

• **French Service**

As everyone eats around the table, we need to set and clear off the table before and after every meal. We have to place the fork, knife, spoon, plates, glass, towels, water, and bread on the table. At the end of the meal, we have to take everything back and clean everything either by hand or with the dishwasher. When they get older, kids and teenagers are asked to do those tasks. They learn that eating is a ritual which requires time, preparation, and organization.

• **Sitting around the table**

Kids learn to sit at the table throughout the meal. During very long family lunch or dinners, kids are usually gathered together in a special area. French meals have different sequences: hors d'oeuvre, main dish, salads, cheese, and finally dessert. Kids have to stay at the table until the main dish. Then they are usually allowed to leave the table and take a break to play together while the adults eat cheese and salads. Then for the desserts, they will be asked to sit back at the table.

• **Eating all kinds of food**

In France, kids are taught to eat every kind of food. It's of course good for the health but it's also a social learning of savoir vivre. Even if nowadays education is more flexible, kids are taught and forced to eat fruits and vegetables and drink water. Even at school, menus change every day and sugary drinks are forbidden.

• No right for dessert

Kids love sugar and desserts. To motivate and force them to eat vegetables during meals, parents use desserts as a reward. In the same way, they use the removal of desserts as a punishment. Every French kid remembers this sentence: «If you dont finish your homework, you won't have dessert! »

• Food is precious

History, famines, and wars taught French people to give importance and value to food. French people don't throw food away. At home, we can recycle meat or vegetables into gratins or soup for example. In the same way, French kids are taught not to waste and throw food away.

• French kids learn to eat with others

From their young age, French kids learn to eat with other people. Kids are never left alone during meal times. Kids always spend their meals with parents at home or others kids at school. So they develop this notion of eating together. Later in the professional life, they usually spend their lunch time with colleagues or friends or even family if they live nearby. Until the development of fast food, French people seldom ate alone in a public space.

WHY EATING TOGETHER IS POSITIVE

- it pushes us to eat slowly or in a different rhythm than alone

- it helps us discover new kinds of food.

- it forces us to pay attention to the quantity of food that we eat.

- inviting persons to eat with us forces us to choose good ingredients and develop better eating habits.

- sharing meals force us to communicate, to exchange ideas, and to laugh.

- pushes us to get out our daily, selfish routine

WHY EATING IN FRONT OF DIGITAL SCREENS IS NOT GOOD

We have to stay concentred on the quantity and
quality of what we eat, otherwise:

• our brain will not be able to judge how much we are
eating, and we might risk overeating, and as a result,
you know what : weight gain.

• if we don't make it a habit to watch what we eat, we
tend to eat less quality food and more junk food and
processed food.

• we will make bad social habits and tend to become
more selfish and less social.

• we don't prepare our body for a good digestion, and
that might result in stomach aches and slow metabolism.

• we won't make eating a main activity, and we will
tend to give less importance to our meals ;
this might result in bad habits and bad food quality.

L'ART DE LA TABLE

The French emphasize so-called « table arts » which are the arts associated with the meals had together, such as cutlery, tableware, and table cloths. It's a big industry, and many professional fairs take place in Paris every year.

In European history, table art became more and more popular through different monarchies. Cutlery, tableware, and tablecloths became more sophisticated. In France, the century of Louis VIV and the extravagance of the Versailles events contributed to this development. Inside aristocratic houses, each room had its proper function. People cook in the kitchen, they eat in the dining room, and they take coffee or tea in the living room.

Until the end of the XIX century, the future bride brought to her future home items from her ancestors called « le trousseau ». It included tablecloths, homemade embroidered bedroom clothes, clothes, cutlery, and tableware …. « Le trousseau » was traditionally prepared by the mother and the grandmother of the future housewife. It was also a symbol of social status and the wealthiness of the family.
Today, tradition has changed and everything is given and ordered by the internet. Meanwhile, we can still find within apartments or houses memories of the past passed on from generations such as sofas, decorations, cutlery.

French people like to invite each other for lunch, afternoon teas, or dinner at home. Being a host and having guests doesn't mean taking care of the food only. Choices of tableware, plates, cutlery, interior design, and even music are part of this ritual. No need to live in a castle to enjoy inviting guests!

Voilà !

Voila, let's be aware that eating is not only putting food and drink into your stomach. This can be a moment of happiness that we can share. We can use this time to take a break and consider it as a real activity. Alone or with others, let's try to create those rituals to enjoy those little, precious daily moments!

Ok, now let's get up, let's go and get a big a glass of water, and let's think about our next meal!

Habit 10

LA VIE EN ROSE

One French secret is to enjoy life and try to increase happiness, especially when we eat. The French consider eating as one of the pleasures of life. Life is short, so we should enjoy it!

POSITIVE SPIRIT vs NEGATIVES FEELINGS

No wonder the two main themes in the French literature are love and the loss of time. The French usually live their everyday life trying to enjoy every moment with passion. Eating is part of it, so we should savor what we eat. When we eat, our body produces hormones inside our blood. Eating is the best anti-anxiety drug ever created! This phenomenon is even emphasized when we eat sugar. This will increase the level of serotonin (the happiness molecule). We should choose what we eat and enjoy those moments rather than bear them.

When we eat junk food, it is maybe because we are starving. We tend to do so when we are moody, bored or stressed. Our negative feelings could potentially lead us to an uncontrolled way of eating. This behavior usually creates weight gain and sometimes even obesity. We should realize that our private relationship troubles or existential crisis wont be solved by eating over-sugary chocolate bars or over-salty potato chips! We shouldn't lose control of our eating habits and become victims of our negative emotions or stress.

HOW FRENCH PEOPLE TRY TO REDUCE STRESS?

Don't take life too seriously

The French use a lot of expressions such as, « it's not that bad ! » or « don't worry, we'll see » . Even if it's not always easy, we have to learn how to put our daily lives into perspective. Anyway, no one can predict the future, so let's try to enjoy every present moment!

Good Food

Eating more fruits and vegetables helps regulate our body in a better way. Let's drink herbal teas which will increase our inner peace and make water our best friend!

Vacations

The French are well-known to live for their vacations. Let's learn to create more free time in our weekly schedule and make the best of it!

Sleep and rest

We have to learn to sleep well. Our body needs to rest. Lack of sleep will lead us to eating added sugar, junk food, and to snacking all morning long.

Love

Let's spread love in our life and around us. Let's be passionate, create, and share good feelings!

Money alone won't bring happiness

We've heard this thousands of times already. Of course, we need money to live. But we shouldn't neglect our private life and time just for money and work. The French don't live to work but work to live and enjoy their free time.

Social Life

Let's push ourselves to find a happy social life: let's meet or call friends, family, and colleagues. Let's exchange ideas and feelings....

Move

Let's move all of our body, so we can be in good shape and make the stress go away!

Laugh

Laughing is good for mental and physical health! Let's watch a funny movie or video, and let's meet friends!

Free Time

Bored? Nothing to do? Let's find a hobby that we like, that we could share with others. Let's learn new things like cooking, foreign languages, and yoga…

Zen attitude

Let's try and learn how to relieve stress and anxiety through relaxation, yoga, meditation, and breathing.

Digital Detox

Let's try to reduce the time we spend in front of our screens and smartphones. When we have a screen open in front of our eyes, our brain is awake, constantly working, and cannot really rest. Stop watching TV one hour before sleeping - disconnect our brain and let our body relax.

16 HAPPY FOODS !

Eating well can lift our mood and bring us joy. Have some foods that make you happy. As always, we need to eat them with moderation and not excess. This is just an indicative list, and we should look for more that can suit us best!

1. **Whole cereals, nuts, almonds**
   These foods are iron, magnesium, and amino acid rich.
   They can be added into salads, meals, and desserts.
   They bring us energy and help us fight against stress
   and tiredness.

2. **Tuna**
   Tuna is good for the health and for our wallet. It can be added in our salads and sandwichs. Omega3 rich, it will makes us happy!

3. **Olive oil**
   Stop buying artificial and chemical salad dressing! Let's use vegetable oils! Olive oil can be used hot to cook or cold as a dressing. It has lots of benefits for the body and

contains antioxidants. It's better to choose cold pressed olive oil, which is high in nutrients and healthy fats.

4. Chia seeds

Chia seeds are loaded with omega 3 and antioxidants. They are one of the best sources of fiber in the world. Perfect to give some crunchy textures to your salads or desserts!

5. Oily Fish

Salmon, mackerel, and sardines are sources of omega 3 fatty acids. They will boost our brain and make us happy.

6. Eggs

Eggs gives us proteins, amino acids, and good cholesterol. They will boost our dopamine and make us feel good. They can be eaten alone or cooked in thousands of ways! They are perfect for breakfast and as healthy snacking !

7. Chicken

Chicken contains tryptophan which will produce serotonin and make us happy. It is rich in protein and good for the heart.

8. Gruyere Cheese

Cheese is another source of tryptophan, especially in gruyere cheese. It can be used everywhere in our food and will make us happy.

9. Sweet Potatoes

They look a bit like potatoes, but are more digestable. They contains fiber, good sugars, and glucose. They boost our immunity and support our digestive system. They can be added in our salads or main meals.

10. Spinach

Spinach is great for health. It has fewer calories and is iron rich. They bring us happiness and energy. Cooked spinach is more easily digestable than raw.

11. Beetroot

Beetroot can be eaten raw or cooked, on its own or mixed in salads. They are great sources of betaine, fiber, vitamine C, and folate. They will lower blood pressure and increase exercise capacity.

12. Honey

Honey has been used as a remedy for long time. Honey contains antioxidants and has antibacterial properties. You can add it anywhere, within salty meals, sugary desserts, or drinks. It's better use raw and unpasteurized honey.

13. Ginger

This plant originated from China and will boost our immune system. It contains antioxidants and has antibacterial properties. Ginger will heat up your body and might even have some aphrodisiac properties.

14. Cinnamon

Cinnamon has been used throughout history as a precious spice. It contains antioxidants and has antiinflammatory properties. It has powerful effects on our health and metabolism. It can be added everywhere in our meals and drinks.

15. Camomille

Chamomile herbal tea will bring you peace, improve our digestion, and helps us sleep.

16. Black Chocolate

We had to finish this tiny list with black chocolate. No one will deny that chocolate makes you happy! It contains very low IG and natural antioxident properties. Perfect with a glass of wine, with moderation of course!

WHY WILL STRESS AFFECT OUR WEIGHT?

Our gut is our second brain. We all experience times of tensions and stress. We know how it can affect our appetite and our digestive system. We all use words and expressions like: bad blood, get butterflies in (one's) stomach, and quit your bellyaching!

Tons of searchers and scientists have proved the relationship between the brain and gut. To try to understand better, let's talk quickly about the vagus nerve and the stress hormone cortisol.

The Vagus Nerve

The vagus nerve is the longest cranial nerve. It passes through the heart, lungs, and digestive tract.
It helps the gut move but it also does much more. It helps the treatment of our emotions through our brain, heart and gut. Specialists think there are millions of neurones inside our gut which informs the vagus nerve and brain on how our stomach and intestines are doing. There is total interaction both ways between brain and gut.
Now we can understand easily why our emotions affect our digestion and vice versa. Our way of eating can interact with our mood in both ways.

Cortisol

Cortisol is our body's main stress hormone. When our environnement induces stress, our body tends to produce cortisol hormones in excess quantities. Cortisol under long term stress periods will lead to increased blood sugar levels. Our body will put itself in danger mode and will start to store energy. The result can be an increase in appetite and can cause cravings for junk foods and of course, undesirable weight gain.

So every time we are under stress or strong emotional situations, our body will tend to lead us to sweet, high-fat, and salty foods. We should learn to live by reducing stress and negative emotions in order to stay in good health.

Voilà !

Life is short, and we have to enjoy it. Let's try to stay positive as much as possible and maybe soon, like Edith Piaf said in her song, we'll see « la vie en rose ».

OK, so now let's take a deep breath, stand up, and stop complaining. Let's look at ourself in a mirror with a big smile. Then let's drink a big glass of water and call a friend while walking a bit! Let's enjoy life!

Santé !

I didn't want to add the wine part in my French secrets selection as my goal is not to force anyone to drink wine. Wine contains, of course, alcohol, and we should drink alcohol with moderation.

By the way, for those who don't drink wine but wanna join in with friends drinking, I recommend buying grape juice. It's non-alcoholic and has quite the same color and texture as wine. Anyway, secret or not, wine is part of French culture. France is continually one the top three countries worldwide in terms of producing and drinking wine. Wine has been a French tradition for centuries and is still very strong in everyday life.

HOW DO THE FRENCH DRINK WINE ?

Be Simple

Tradition, education, and strong wine production makes wine the alcoholic beverage most likely to be had with everyday meals. The French consider beer to not be an appropriate drink for meals, and the French seldom drink beer while eating. We choose wine by experience or by asking for advice from family, friends, and sellers…. Sharing a bottle makes it very user friendly. Forget the stereotype; no need to be sommelier to enjoy drinking wine!

Break Time

For the French, drinking wine is also a moment to have a break. It's a transition between work and rest. It's a time to slow down and reconnect oneself with the agriculture world and wineries. It's a moment to share with colleagues, friends, family….

When someone invites you to eat at their home, you should bring a gift. It's usually either flowers or a bottle of wine, or both. The French like to buy some wine in advance and let it get old.

When we celebrate a big event, we drink a special bottle we've kept for long time or an expensive one.

At home, there is no need to be a big connoisseur to appreciate and share the wine ritual. Before opening the bottle, we can enjoy looking the label and checking the color and aspects of the bottle. Then we open the bottle with a corkscrew. Then we taste the wine using many senses, such as sight, smell, and taste…. This is a unique experience and opens up many talking points around it.

Consumption Mode

Wine is generally drunk during meals or at aperitif time.
In restaurants, we can generally order wine by bottle or by glass.

Cheaper wines can even be ordered by carafe. If you stop by at a café, you can drink a glass of wine at the counter.
We can also drink wine during aperitif. Wine diversity allows everyone to enjoy and choose favorites.

Santé

Drinking alcohol is first of all a synonym of free time and sharing. The French use the word "santé" during a toast. It's amazing because "santé" means "health" in French. There are different origins or explanations to this. Some say that wine can make you sleep and rest, so it's good for health. Others say that they consider drinking alcohol as a spiritual ritual so that they stay connected with life and health. But the main reason to toast and stay healthy was to make sure you could trust your partners or relationships. By clinking glasses with each other, drinks mixed together and everybody drank from the same source, being sure there was no poison inside.

PETIT WINE HISTORY

Wine has a long history, and we'll need books to describe the whole wine history.

In Europe, Greek and Roman civilizations developed the traditions and agriculture of wine. At the end of the Roman Empire, the catholic church received the quasi monopoly of the culture of wine. Wine was drunk during religious ceremonies, and churches and monks owned most of the wineries. Still today, some famous French wines have kept the Christian name of the wine such as: Saint Emilion, Saint Joseph, etc… ("saint" means holy in French).

Most people will recognize the name Dom Perignon, who contributed to the development of a special sparkling wine, which will become champagne later on.

At this time, white and rose wines were the most popular. We will have to wait until the Middle Ages to see the development of red wine.

Later, discovery of the new world by European kingdoms such as Spain, Italy, and France expanded wineries worldwide. We can now find old French and European grape varieties in South Africa, Australia, and even California with a Franciscan monk heritage.

GEOGRAPHIC ORIGIN

- ## AOC

Wineries are defined by territory. Most of them take their name from their geography. The first official wine classification starts in the beginning of the XXs and classifies wine by region. For example, names like Bordeaux, Bourgogne, Loire, Alsace, Beaujolais, and Champagne are names of a cities or French regions that come before the name of the wine.

The AOC "appellation d 'origine controlée, or origin controlled label, means that a wine produced in a specific area cannot be produced anywhere else. There must be a link between wine characteristics and the origin of its production. Moreover, to get this label, the wine has to fit strict criteria, such as: alcohol degree, process of fabrication, grape variety choice….

Because of this, we cannot call a wine produced out of the Champagne area a Champagne.

• **Le Champagne**

In France, for 1000 years, most of the kings' ceremonies took place in the cathedral of Reims, a city located 100 km northeast of Paris in the heart of the area called Champagne. During those ceremonies, kings gathered for extraordinary meals where wines of the area were served. Those wines became very popular among all European kingdoms. A symbol of exception and luxury, champagne has kept its reputation throughout the years all over the world. Nowadays, champagne is still synonymous with special events for French people.

• **Le Beaujolais Nouveau**

The beaujolais nouveau is a wine produced in the winery of the area of Beaujolais northern Lyon and south of Macon.

Let's do a quick history lesson. In 1951, a new French law allowed wine producers to release wines of the year from the 15th of December of the same year. Some wineries from the Beaujolais area started to revolt because they wanted to release their wine before that date. After negotiations, they won the battle and were allowed to commercialize their new wine earlier under the label "nouveau." That's how Beaujolais Nouveau was born.

After years of marketing, this mini local revolution created one of the most exported wines in France. Every year, people celebrate Beaujolais Nouveau, the 3rd Thursday of November, in more than 100 countries around the world.

It is nice timing, since it's celebrated between summer and end of the year!

GRAPEWINES

Grape varieties are the base of the wine. Wine production depends on many factors, such as quality of the soil, weather, and area.

Most of the grapes used for wine have white flesh. This is the grape wine maceration mixed with the skins, which will give the wine its color.

7 popular grapewines in the world

1. Cabernet sauvignon (rouge)

Born in Bordeaux area in France, this is one of the most planted in the world. It gave birth to the big Bordeaux names but also a lot of wines of the new world: Napa Valley, Australia, South Africa, Argentina….

You can find it in French wines such as: Médoc

2. Merlot (rouge)

This is the main grape used for red wine production in France, especially in the Bordeaux area. You can find it in French wines such as: Chateau Petrus

3. Grenache noir (rouge)

Born in Spain, you can find it in Rhone and southwest French wines. Its taste is strong, high in alcohol, and flavored.

Example: Côtes du Rhône

4. Syrah (rouge)

Born in Northern Rhone area in France, you can also find it in
Provence and Languedoc wines. It's very popular in the new
world, especially in Australia.
You can find it in French wines such as: Côte rôtie

5. Pinot noir (rouge)

Born in the Burgundy area in France, you can also find it in
many Alsace and Loire wine. One of the most planted in the
world.
You can find it in French wine such as: Romanée-Conti

6. Sauvignon (blanc)

Born between the Loire and Bordeaux regions of France, it
produces liquored as well as dry white wines.
You can find it in French wines such as: Sancerre

7. Chardonnay (blanc)

This is the most famous white grape in the world. It can adapt
in a lot of soil and produce wine easily. It produces the most
popular wine in USA.
You can find it in French wine such as: Chablis

HOW TO MATCH WINE AND MEALS ?

Wine matching well with all dishes but it is sometimes difficult to choose. First of all, don't hesitate to ask the advice of your wine reseller.
Here are the basic French rules:

red meats
match well with stronger red wines

red and white meat dishes
match well with lighter red wines

hors d'oeuvres and fish
match well with stronger white wine

seafood and shellfish
match well with dry and sparkling white wines

white meat and poultry
match well with white wines

sweet dishes and desserts
match well with sparking and sweet white wines

Rosé wine was mostly served in summer but is becoming more and more popular all year long.

Champagne is mostly served in aperitif or dessert for special occasions. The French seldom eat a whole meal with champagne.

LE FRENCH PARADOX

Anglo Saxons have defined the "French paradox" as the paradox between the French way of eating heavily-buttered cuisine and drinking wine with the good public health statistics of French people.
A lot of international studies show that wine can have beneficial effects on our body and health.
Wine has a lot of antioxidants and could help with heart problems and cholesterol levels.

Organic wine is even better for our body. It is becoming more and more popular in Europe. France is in the top three countries in the world where organic wine is produced. Organic wine is more selective in its fabrication process, such as no usage of chemical products with respect to the ground and fields. These productions are smaller than the classic wines, but they are becoming more and more popular with the public.

CONSUME WITH MODERATION

I must remind you that alcohol should be drunk with moderation.
We shouldn't drink more than one or two glasses of wine max per day. Pregnant women are not advised to drink alcohol. Let's finish by reminding that excess alcohol consumption can result in several troubles and also disease.

A last point: we should know that when we drink, alcohol will affect our brains and our sensations.
We might lose the sensation of getting full when we eat. So if we drink a lot, we might eat more than usual, so you know what

might happen next....
So let's drink, but in a responsible and positive way!

Voilà !

OK, let's stand up and go drink a big glass of water! It s not yet to time for aperitif!

Santé!

Some studies reference showing correlation between wine consumption and health benefits.

Explaining the French paradox
Michael L Burr
Centre for Applied Public Health Medicine University of Wales
College of Medicine Cardiff
Journal of the Royal Society of Health, Volume: 115 issue: 4,
page(s): 217-219
Issue published: August 1, 1995

Impact of Red Wine Consumption on Cardiovascular Health
Author(s): Luca Liberale, Aldo Bonaventura, Fabrizio Montecucco*,
Franco Dallegri, Federico Carbone
Journal Name: Current Medicinal Chemistry
Volume 26 , Issue 19 , 2019

Red Wine Consumption and Cardiovascular Health
by Luigi Castaldo 1,2, Alfonso Narváez 1, Luana Izzo 1, Giulia
Graziani 1, Anna Gaspari 1, Giovanni Di Minno 2 and Alberto
Ritieni
University of Naples, Italy

Wine, alcohol, platelets, and the French paradox for coronary heart disease
S. Renaud, PhD , M. de Lorgeril, MD
Published:June 20, 1992

French Dishes

For centuries, France has been a country mainly based on agriculture. The emblem of France is still the Gallic Rooster. Most of French dishes come from different areas of France. They all have all different specification regarding the local animal or vegetable production. Each region is proud of its local treasures, and this is what develops the diversity of our dishes. UNESCO has even declared French cuisine an "intangible cultural heritage." So, I had to write this small list of the most famous French dishes. Unfortunately, I cannot mention all the dishes here. But here is a small selection of our national treasures. Let's start with the symbol of France: la baguette.

- **LA BAGUETTE**

Bread existed in France for centuries. Its process has been regulated and ruled by authorities since the Middle Ages. Originally, bread was made in a form of miche or boule. The stick shape called "baguette" appeared in the 19th century. Years later, it became more and more popular in Paris. As the baguette is made in a smaller quantity, it pushed French people to buy it everyday. It stays the most eaten type of bread in France and the symbol of the nation worldwide.

SOME FRENCH DISHES

• LA RATATOUILLE

Originally from Mediterranean south coast, this dish is a vegetable stew with olive oil. Ratatouille is uses Provence vegetables, such as tomatoes, zucchinis, eggplants, peppers, onions, and herbs like thyme or parsley.

• LE CASSOULET

This stew from south west France mixes white beans and a set of confit meats, such as duck and sausage.

• L'ALIGOT

Aligot comes from Aveyron. This is mashed potatoes and slim slices of Tome cheese, butter, cream, and crushed garlic. We serve it hot with a long spoon, allowing the melted cheese to create long strings. We eat it generally with beef and sausage.

• LA BOUILLABAISSE

Bouillabaisse is a southern specialty from Marseilles and Mediterranean cuisine. At first, this stew was made from fish leftovers that fisherman couldn't sell at the daily market.
Today, we say we need at least 4 different fish to prepare it. This

brown-colored fish soup comes with croutons and "rouille" (a homemade sauce like mustard with garlic, saffron, and olive oil). With it, we cook a mix of vegetables and herbs. It is usually served in two different dishes: one for the soup and one for the fish.

• LA CHOUCROUTE

"Choucroute" meant first compost cabbage. It is prepared with cabbage that cut into slices. The cabbage is served with salted meats, sausages, and potatoes. This dish is very popular in east France, Alsace. We eat it with Alsace white wine or beer.

• LA RACLETTE

In Auvergne, the center France and close to Switzerland, there are lot of dishes, such as RACLETTE made from melted cheese and an assortment of delicatessen.

• LE CROQUE MONSIEUR

This is the Parisian bistro classic: the French hamburger! This dish is made with slices of ham and cheese inserted into two slices of soft bread. Everything is toasted on demand. It usually comes with French fries or a salad.

• LE POT AU FEU

Le pot au feu is a beef stew with vegetables. It is made from various pieces of beef with bone marrow and a lot of vegetables such as carrots, leeks, potatoes, onions, and a bouquet garnish.

• LE GRATIN DAUPHINOIS

This dish originated from the Dauphiné region in southeastern France. It is made of sliced potatoes, baked in milk or cream.

• LA FONDUE SAVOYARDE

This is a melting pot made that has white wine and cheese from Savoie area. It is cooked inside a communal pot, and everyone can dip a piece of bread with a long special knife into the melted cheese. This is more like a winter dish and very friendly to share.

• LE BOEUF BOURGUIGNON

This famous beef burgundy is from the Bourgogne area. We can find the products to make it from Bourgogne area, like the wine and the beef. It is a beef stewed and braised in red wine with carrots, mushrooms, potatoes, and garlic. It is cooked slowly for a long time so the wine flavor soaks into the meat.
La particularité est sa cuisson lente qui laisse bien le vin imprégner la viande.

• LES ESCARGOTS

Despite this worldwide reputation, the French seldom eat snails. We can find them sometimes on the menu of family gatherings or tourist restaurants. Traditionally, snails were boiled and put back inside their shell with garlic and parsley butter. Then the whole preparation is put into the oven. Today, it's easy to buy them already prepared. To eat them, we need a special utensil: a long, thin fork. Snails are usually a dish for tourists, and they are still served in French bistros. We order them generally by 6 at a time.

• LA SOUPE A L'OIGNON

This famous French onion soup will warm your stomach and heart. It is still a Parisian brasserie classic dish for the late nighters. It is served with a toasted baguette slice called a "crouton" and melted cheese.

- ### LE COQ AU VIN

This may be one the most famous French dishes in the world. Originally, this dish was created by farmers to use old roasters with tougher meat. It is cooked in a red wine sauce with onions, carrots, mushrooms, and a small piece of bacon.

- ### LE STEAK TARTARE

This is one of the Parisian bistro classics. This dish is a raw beef steak cut in big pieces with a knife. It is mixed with many ingredients, such as an egg, spices, sauces. It comes with French fries and salad.

- ### LE CONFIT DE CANARD

Specialty from southwest France, duck is cooked in its own fat, and it is generally served with duck-fat fried potatoes. A must taste!

- ### LES CUISSES DE GRENOUILLE

Even if frog legs are one of the most heard international stereotypes regarding the French, this dish is hard to find nowadays. Frogs legs are prepared in flour and mixed with garlic and parsley and then pan fried. You can now find this dish frozen and already pre-prepared.

- ### LA QUICHE

Served from the 16th century, this pie is a classic home recipe. Bacon, cream, cheese, and eggs make this baked, delicious savory pie. We can eat it cold or hot, in hors d'oeuvre or as amain dish. It usually comes with raw vegetables or a salad. Very popular at home or in bistro lunch menu, this is the French's pizza. We can add all kinds of garnishes on top.

• LES MOULES FRITES

Mussels and French fries! This dish is very popular around the French coast, but you can also find it in brasseries. Mussels are cooked in a white wine broth with shallots and parsley. They come with French fries.

• LE LAPIN A LA MOUTARDE

The French have always been big rabbit consumers. Nowadays, this rabbit habit is not so common. One of the most popular recipes is rabbit in a dijon mustard sauce served with potatoes or rice.

• LE FOIE GRAS

Often criticized in the international scene for its production process, foie gras paté is a must during the French end of year meals. It is commonly served as starter with a sugary wine and garnished with sea salt.

• LA TRUFFE

France is one of the main producers of this famous mushroom. Truffle prices can reach up to hundreds of dollars depending on their size, types, and quality. It is really a luxury product. It is often used mixed with other ingredients or as a topping on special dishes.

SOME FRENCH DESSERTS

• LE CROISSANT

The croissant was born in Vienna, Austria. Marie Antoinette brought the recipe with her when she moved to Versailles. Later on, French bakeries reworked it and created butter croissants in the beginning of last century. This is a classic of French snack or breakfast. You can find it in every French bakery!

• LA MADELEINE

Originally from Spain, this small cake is a pastry classic and became popular from the writings of Marcel Proust. Easy recognized with its shell shape, it can be long or round. It can have many flavors or colors, but the butter version is the original one.

• LE PROFITEROLE

This is a dessert created with choux pastry and made with butter, flour, water, and eggs. It is filled with a cream or vanilla glaze and served with a hot melted chocolate topping.

• LE CANELE

This French pastry is flavored with rum and vanilla and has a caramelized crust. It's soft on the inside and crispy on the outside. It has this particular cylindrical shape due to the cylindrical mold used to bake it.

• LA TARTE TATIN

As one legend says, the Tatin sisters created this pie. They cooked in their restaurant, and their specialty was apple pie. One day, one sister forgot to add dough in the mold and by accident created the "tarte Tatin". Apples are caramelized in butter and sugar before the tart is baked. It is usually served with cream or vanilla ice cream.

• LE MACARON

Macarons have existed for centuries in Europe. A French pastry chef offered some in the wedding of Louis XIV. At first, it was just a single round dry cookie. Later, it was assembled into two parts and garnished with spices. This small cake is made of almond, sugar, and egg and is now a favorite element of afternoon tea around the world.

- **LA CREME BRULEE**

This is French dessert is composed of eggs, vanilla bean, and caramelized sugar on top. It is a classic dessert in every bistro and brasserie.

- **LES CREPES**

Created in west France, in Bretagne, crepes are one of the most popular desserts in the world. The so-called crepes are prepared with regular flour and is usually sweet. The so-called "galette" versions are prepared with buckwheat flour. They are thicker and are mostly savory. They can be prepared in infinite variations. It's a very popular dish at home.

The list could go on and on with quatre quart, fruit tarts, clafoutis, far breton etc, etc...

SOME FRENCH CHEESE

- **LE CAMEMBERT**

Camembert is the number one cheese we associate with France. Originally from Normandy, it has the same name as the village Camembert.
Only camembert cheese produced in France is true A.O.C. Camembert de Normandie.

- **LA BUCHETTE DE CHEVRE**

There are a lot kind different kinds of goat cheeses, and the buchette is one of the most popular. The French love it and use some soft versions in their salads and sandwiches.

• L'EMMENTAL, LE GRUYERE

Do not mistake the French gruyere for the Swiss counterpart. It is a milk-based cheese made in Savoie and Franche Comte. The Swiss one is easy recognizable with the big holes on its surface.

• LE ROQUEFORT

Roquefort is one of the best-known blue cheeses. It's a sheep milk cheese from south France. It has very distinctive blue veins on its mold.

• LE COMTE

This cow's milk cheese comes from the Franche Comté region of eastern France. This is a classic French cheese and looks similar to the French Gruyere.

• LE BRIE

Brie could be the ancestor of soft cheeses. It's a very creamy cheese, softer than camembert. It has a large diameter with white rind on the outside.

• LE REBLOCHON

Reblochon is a cheese made in the French Savoy region from raw cow's milk. We can eat it alone, with cheese dishes, or in potatoes gratin.

• LE SAINT NECTAIRE

This is a cheese made in the Auvergne region of central France, and it is made of cow's milk. It has a grey appearance.

•   **LE MUNSTER**

Munster is a soft and smelly cheese from the Vosges region, made from raw cow's milk.

•   **LE BROCCIU**

Produced in Corsica, the Brocciu is the only cheese made with goat or ewe's milk.

Needless to say, this is a small selection, because France has the largest number of cheeses in the world!

This whole list is far from exhaustive. There are a ton of guides about French regional food.

Let's finish with one of the most popular guides in the world:
the Michelin Guide.

Originally, the Michelin brothers ran a tire company during the beginning of the last century. The first guide they produced was a free commercial guidebook given to their clients with a list of doctors, auto garages, and local tourist spots. But when they didn't sell enough tires, they created a new guide with more tourist places to visit, as well as restaurants. With this, they hoped new drivers would drive longer distances and have the need to purchase more tires. The guide kept growing, both nationally and internationally. Despite growing controversies, the guide continues to give stars to restaurants.

Now you know everything!

Voilà !

After this mise en bouche, we allow you taste the French treasures from all regions! Enjoy your tour de France and Bon appetit!

FIN

The goal of balancing what we eat is not to lose a huge amount of weight in a short period of time. We have to accept our body and find a way to live in harmony. There is no perfect body, and we shouldn't try to compete with anybody. We all know that we didn't choose our genetic heritage, but we can always improve our habit to become healthier!

IT'S NEVER TOO LATE TO CHANGE

We are all able to change. We just need to be honest with ourselves and find courage to jump into the water. Before starting anything, let's study ourselves to learn our own habits. What are we looking for? What goal do we want to reach? What kind of behavior can we improve? What bad habits can we replace?

STEP BY-STEP

We are all creatures of habit. We create our lifestyle routine by minimizing our intellectual and physical efforts. Let's think about small changes to improve our way of eating. Changing even just a few habits can make big results! Let's try to change our tune and make positive habits such as: eating at the same time of day, preparing a bottle of water to take with you during your day, buying healthy snacks, and planning our shopping.

After all, there are no big risks in buying more fruits and vegetables instead of junk food!

POSITIVE FUTURE

Don't put too much pressure on yourself! Don't aim for dramatic changes in a short amount time. We have to think new habits on the long term. Let's try to build better rhythms with our life and eating habits.

Be curious, and try to test and learn new things each day. We have our whole lives to reach our goal! Let's think positively every morning by thinking how we can change not only our life, but our loved one's lives as well! Let's try to be positive, especially when we are in a blue mood.

TO BE CONTINUED ...

Thank you so much for taking the time to read this book.
I hope this will bring you helpful tips and tricks and give you some ideas to improve your way of eating and help you feel better every day.

So, let's stand up, let's grab a big glass of water, and add some vegetables to our shopping list! Let's call some friends and plan a lunch or dinner together!

Let's enjoy life, which can be so beautiful if we decide to make it that way!